Live Now, Die Later

Copyright © 2018 by Nicole L. Turner

All rights reserved. No part of this publication may be reproduced, distributed, or transmitted in any form or by any means, including photocopying, recording, or other electronic or mechanical methods, without the prior written permission of the publisher, except in the case of brief quotations embodied in critical reviews and certain other noncommercial uses permitted by copyright law.

Printed in the United States of America

First Printing, 2018

ISBN-13: 978-0988756915
ISBN-10: 0988756919

Live Now, Die Later: Stop Trying to Fit into a Box that Wasn't Created for You

Nicole L. Turner

The Detox Strategist™

www.detoxstrategist.com

Also by Nicole L. Turner

Detox Your Life: Building a Healthy Relationship with Yourself and Others

Toxic Work Environment eBook

Detox Your Relationship: Know When to Stay and When to Let Go

https://www.amazon.com/Nicole-L.-Turner/e/B00U681N02

"To live is the rarest thing in the world. Most people just exist." ~ Oscar Wilde

"Life has no limitations, except the ones you make." ~ Les Brown

"The saddest summary of a life contains three descriptions: could have, might have, and should have." ~ Louis E. Boone

"Ten years from now, make sure you can say you chose your life, you didn't settle for it." ~ Author Unknown

Introduction

One of the scariest feelings that any person can have is that they are just moving through life and not actually living their life. They are just existing, but not really living. Are you living life by default and not by design? Many people feel as though they are just going through the motions and are not actually experiencing what it is like to be alive. They have just accepted whatever has been thrown at them. It's time to live now and die later.

In this book, I will share tips on ways to live life now. As with my other books, I am just having a conversation with you; hence, the reason why there's no table of contents. I want you, the reader, to be able to open the book to any page and gain something from the reading. This book also has a 21-days activity to help you live your best life now.

A plot twist can happen at any time in your life.

Perhaps previous months or years haven't gone the way you had hoped. Don't get discouraged. As we see often, things and life can change in the blink of an eye. But I must be honest, perhaps one of the reasons things haven't gone the way you thought it would is because you have been living a life of default.

When you get a new cell phone, tablet, or computer, do you stick with the default settings or do you change the settings to your personal preferences? Most people change the settings. When you live a life by default, you are basically accepting what's already been selected for you. We all know people who seem to experience the same set of challenges or obstacles over and over again, or who have the same or similar negative life events happen to them, regardless of where they are or what they are doing. You are a co-creator of your experiences and when you have internal stress, frantic pressure, and a doom or gloom mentality, your life reflects that back to you.

There's a quote that says, "If you don't live a life by design, you will live a life by default." Living life by default means that you are just passively accept things the way life is showing up for you. Here are some ways to tell if you are living life by default: (1) Do you constantly have a feeling that something is missing? (2) Are major aspects of your life decided by happenstance – things like your what you do on a daily basis, your career, your friends, your dating life, etc.? (3) Do you wake up each day and feel like you are simply reacting to what life is throwing at you? (4) You have no idea of what will truly make you happy. If you answered yes, you may be living a life by default.

Here are five tips to help you live a life by design instead of living a life by default:

- Get clear about what you really want out of life. That means defining what makes YOU happy.
- Now that you are clear about what you really want out of life, create a life plan. That means setting goals and achieving them. They don't have to be big audacious goals. People think that their goals have to be something big to make a difference, and when they don't reach the big goal, they feel unhappy, stressed, depressed or out of alignment. Small goals are just as important. It's that practice of achieving the small goals that lead to even bigger goals. Achieving small goals build confidence to aim higher.

- You need purpose. Your purpose is your why. It's that "thing" that makes your life fulfilling. It's something that resonates deeply within your heart.

- Learn to be in the moment. According to a Harvard University study, almost half of our waking hours are spent NOT living in the moment. Half! Living in the moment is also associated with mindfulness. Mindfulness is the ability to be fully present, aware of where you are and what you're doing, and not overly reactive or overwhelmed by what's going on around you.

- Live a life of gratitude. I will **ALWAYS** emphasize the importance of being grateful. Gratitude makes us happier. Research shows that gratitude increases mental strength, strengthens our emotions, increases our self-esteem, reduces aggression, improves psychological health, and improves physical health.

Have you ever been so close, but so far?

As I continue on this journey called life, trying to figure it all out...connect the dots, I can actually see the number of times I was so close, but yet so far. So close to that actual breakthrough – that one thing that was going to catapult me into success (my own personal definition of what success looks like for me). It was so close that I could almost reach out and touch it, but in the very center of my blinking eye, it appeared so far away.

I've had the opportunity to share a stage or be interviewed with people I now see on Primetime TV or in magazines or with hundreds of thousands of followers on social media. I mean like we were, at some point in time, on equal playing fields, but when they pulled back on their slingshot, they landed in the RIGHT place at the Right time. I pulled back on my slingshot, and it's as if it was broken.

Have you ever been so close to that ONE thing…you know THAT thing, but it seemed like the Universe was teasing you? You could visualize it. You could darn near taste it, but you just could never seem to be able to hold it in your hands. I have experienced this in various areas of my life: my career, my business, my romantic relationships, my finances. I would find myself saying, "This was almost it, so I know the next one will be It", but ummm the next one wasn't it. It's hard to not get discouraged, especially when you see other people thriving, but you seem to be standing still.

I want to share a few tips with you that will help you stay encouraged and make you unstoppable:

- **Don't be motivated by something external** (e.g., money, fancy things, prestige, etc.). There are people with money, big houses, fancy cars, etc., but they are still miserable on the inside. Yes, they keep pushing themselves to get the things society tells them they should have, but the light within them is dim. Stay true to who you are, and use the gifts and talents YOU were blessed with. Live life on YOUR terms.
- **Remember CONFIDENCE is your greatest strength.** If you're not confident, you will never put yourself out there in the first place. When you're confident, you don't care how many times you fail, you're going to succeed. And it doesn't matter how stacked the odds seem against you.

- **Always be prepared.** Become a master of your craft.
- **Always work on your mental strength.** "Mental resilience is arguably the most critical trait of a world-class performer. ~ Josh Waitzkin
- **Never be jealous or envious of someone else's accomplishments**. Being unstoppable means you genuinely want what's best for everyone—even those you would consider your competitors. Jealousy and envy are the ego, which operates out of fear. You are in control of you and you are different from every other person. There is no one who can do exactly what you can do. You have your own superpower with your own unique ability to contribute, and that's what you're going to do.
- **Start before you're ready.** Most people wait. They believe they can start after they have enough time,

money, connections and credentials. They wait until they feel "secure." Not people who are unstoppable. Unstoppable people started last year. They started five years ago before they even knew what they were doing. They started before they had any money. They started before they had all the answers. They started when no one else believed in them. The only permission they needed was the voice inside them prompting them to move forward, and they moved.

- **Set goals that far exceed your current capabilities**. If your goals are logical, they won't force you to create luck. Being unstoppable means your goals challenge you to be someone more than you currently are. As Jim Rohn has said, *"Don't wish it was easier, wish you were better."*

Another notable by Paul Arden, *"You need to aim beyond what you are capable of. You need to develop a complete disregard for where your abilities end. If you think you're unable to work for the best company in its sphere, make that your aim. If you think you're unable to be on the cover of TIME magazine, make it your business to be there. Make your vision of where you want to be a reality. Nothing is impossible."*

- **Respond immediately, rather than analyzing and stalling.** Just do it. Train yourself to respond immediately when you feel you should do something. Stop questioning yourself. Don't analyze it. Don't question if it came from God or from yourself. Just act. You'll figure out what to do *after* you've taken action. Until you take action, it will all be hypothetical. But once you act, it becomes practical.

Richard Branson said it best, "If somebody offers you an amazing opportunity but you are not sure you can do it, say yes – then learn how to do it later!"

- **Never stop learning.** Ordinary people seek entertainment. Extraordinary people seek education and learning. When you want to become the best at what you do, you never stop learning. You never stop improving and honing your skills and knowledge.

Tips were extracted from the article, "30 Behaviors that will make you Unstoppable"

You may not end up where you thought you were going, but you always end up where you were meant to be.

We all have plans for our life – the type of career we are going to have, the type of mate we will marry, where we are going to live, how many kids we are going to have, etc., but sometimes life doesn't pan out exactly the way we thought.

When I was in high school, I said I wanted to be a lawyer. I went to college, I majored in English. My last year of college, I took the LSAT (law school admissions test), got a pretty decent score, started applying to law school, and then something hit me – was this really what I wanted to do or was it what was expected of me. So needless, to say, I didn't go to law school, but I had no idea what I wanted to do next. I worked a couple of jobs after college – none of which had the potential to lead to an actual career.

One day, I decided I was going to leave Mississippi. Mind you, I had no plan and no money. Just a desire. I went to Atlanta for about two weeks – wasn't for me. Then I drove to the Washington, DC area – mind you, I had no plan, no money, no job, no family, no friends, and really no place to live. Funny, how the decisions we make in our mid 20s are very different from the decisions we would make 10, 15 years later.

I'm not going to go into a long story of how my life has unfolded as a result of me taking a totally different path from the one I had planned in high school. Oh, I must say this, I had ideas of what I thought my life would be once I got settled in the DC area, and let me tell ya, the reality doesn't match the plan.

Okay, now on to you.

Sometimes you have a plan for your life, but God has a different plan for you. Yes, you may have mapped it all out, and could actually visualize it, but all it takes is ONE thing to completely change the trajectory of your life, but as you reflect back on the journey, you see how all the pieces of the puzzle fit together. The person you married is nothing like the person you thought you would marry, but he/she is the best person for you. The career you have is not the one you went to school for, but it fulfills you – it gives you joy.

There are so many aspects of your life that may not have gone or may not go as YOU planned, but they worked out or are working out for YOUR good. It's VERY important for you to be open to the fact that YOUR plan may not be HIS plan. You may not end up where you thought you were going, but you always end up where you were meant to be.

Don't Fall Back into Depression

According to statistics, the depression rate increases around certain times of the year. It is referred to as seasonal depression or seasonal affective disorder (SAD). It has been said that the onset of SAD coincides with shorter days and longer, dark nights. But as we know, depression doesn't just occur during the Winter months. It can happen at any time.

Focusing on your burdens instead of your blessings can leave you feeling stressed, tired, depressed, and physically ill. Focusing on your blessings instead of your burdens helps you avoid depression.

Here are five tips to help you focus more on your blessings:

- **Start your day quietly in prayer.** Wake up a little earlier each morning to spend a few minutes in prayer. Starting your day with prayer or reading a devotional sets the tone for your day.

- **See every moment as a blessing.** I often say, "Any day above ground is a good day." Each day that you are here on this earth is another day to turn a negative into a positive. That means also giving thanks for the "small" blessings. Some people don't recognize a blessing unless it is something bold and big. That day you were in traffic and you were frustrated with the car in front of you because the driver was in the left lane driving like he/she was in a funeral procession, but as you progressed on your route, you saw a bad accident that happened just minutes earlier. Putting that slow driver in your path was a blessing. That job that you just had to have – you know the one you thought was a perfect fit for you, but you didn't get it. Months later, you find out they had massive layoffs or the person you would have been working for is a horrible boss, which would've made your life a living hell. Not getting the job was a blessing.

- **Keep a gratitude log.** There's a quote by Henry Ward Beecher that says, "The unthankful heart discovers no mercies; but the thankful heart will find, in every hour, some heavenly blessings." There is a direct link between our gratitude and our overall well-being. If you start to feel sad or depressed, pause and write down three things you're grateful for. Keep a list on your phone, your computer, or in a handwritten journal.

- **Change your focus.** We tend to focus on the negative aspects of our lives and we forget the blessings that we all have. When you change your attitude to one of counting your blessings you will find you will experience less stress.

- **Be mindful of what you read, watch, listen to, and who you hang around.** What you take in has a great impact on your mental health. Watching the news can be depressing. Watching TV shows with a lot of drama can lead to feelings of stress. Hanging around people who are always negative, critical or in a "woe is me" state of mind have an impact on you mentally.

1 Corinthians 2:9, "What no eye has seen, what no ear has heard, and what no human mind has conceived the things God has prepared for those who love him"

Have you experienced a moment in your life when you were going through something and you just couldn't see your way out? Were you feeling discouraged? Was your faith fading? It's at that moment when you should reflect back on past times in your life when you had that same feeling. Didn't God make a way? When you felt like things were not going to change, didn't they change?

There was a song the choir used to sing at my home church in Mississippi; it goes a little something like this, "As I look back over my life and I think things over, I can truly say that I've been blessed, I've got a testimony. Sometimes I couldn't see my way through, but the Lord, He brought me out; right now I'm free, I've got the victory, I've got a testimony."

God has a plan for your life. Every door you wanted open that He closed was for your good. Every relationship you wanted to work, but it failed, God knew you deserved better. That job you thought was the job for you, but you weren't selected, God is saying that job limits you. That house you wanted, but the contract fell through, God is saying I have a better house for you. That purchase you wanted to make, but something blocked it. That was God saying, "buying it now will put you in a worst situation later." TRUST that when you don't get what you think you want, God has something better and higher for you. Every obstacle, stumbling block, disappointment…was preparing you for bigger and better. Don't allow temporary situations keep you from stepping, leaping…jumping into your destiny. What God has for you is GREATER than you could ever imagine.

Stop Feeding Your History

"Stop feeding your history – don't feed the betrayal. don't feed the hurt. If you needed them, God wouldn't have let them leave. Don't put a question mark where God has put a period. Don't keep mourning over something you cannot change – always thinking about it, wondering why it didn't work out. When you quit putting energy into your history and start putting it into your destiny, God will give you beauty for those ashes."

When I heard Joel Osteen say those words, I instantly thought, "It's the replay that gets you." You spend so much time replaying the scenario over and over in your head, and some of you probably tell it over and over to your family and/or friends. There's a quote I really like that says, "Don't be afraid to lose what was never meant to be." Oh, here's one more quote, "Sometimes He blesses us not in what He gives us, but what He takes away."

Some of you are putting a question mark where God put a period. You are preventing yourself from moving forward because you REFUSE to let go of the past. You keep hitting the mental rewind button as if it's a good movie you want to continuously replay. Stop watering things that were never meant to grow in your life. Bishop T.D. Jakes said it best when he said, "Stop wasting water on dead issues, dead relationships, and a dead past. No matter how much you water concrete, you can't grow a garden." Stop feeding your history!

If you don't sacrifice for what You want, what you want will be the sacrifice

A lot of people say they want this or they want that, but they aren't willing to do what it takes to get what they want. If you're constantly making goals, but not achieving them, there's a disconnect between your desires and your actions. It's time to make some changes.

Perhaps your goal is to quit your job and start a new business – well, we all know that takes a certain level of financial security. The first step may be to work your side hustle while you're working your full-time job to build up your bank account. The second step may be to cut back on eating out or shopping or whatever your "thing" is. Do forensics on your bank account to see what you spend money on each month and then decide what's necessity and what's "nice to haves" & limit the "nice to haves".

Maybe your goal is to get healthier. A healthy lifestyle definitely takes a lot of discipline. Perhaps the first thing you should consider is turning off the TV, cancelling the cable bill. It's so easy to plop down on the couch and watch TV. As we all know, binge eating happens in front of the TV. Take the time you used to watch your favorite TV show and get moving. Okay, if you can't completely give up the TV, while you are watching your favorite TV show, exercise during commercial breaks (e.g., do situps, pushups, squats, jumping jacks, jump rope, etc.).

You want to become debt free. I'm going to repeat some of what I said in a previous paragraph. Identify areas where you are wastefully spending, and make a conscious effort to apply the wastefully spending money to debt. So, what if you can't hang out with your friends as much as you want or buy those new pair of jeans you just have to have. What's more important to you – a temporary "feel good" or financial freedom and knowing that long gone are the days of stressing and worrying about money.

Maybe your goal is to find love – then I suggest you do a self-assessment. Reflect back on the common behaviors/patterns that were evident in if not all, most of your relationships. Ask yourself what unresolved issues are you carrying around. What baggage do you need to let go of? Some of your issues may require therapy. Guess what, therapy is NOT a bad thing. If you are serious about finding love, it starts with self-love and being the best version of you that you can be for yourself. Also, stop being driven by loneliness. So many people end up in unhealthy relationships because of loneliness. So, what if you don't have a date on Friday night. So, what if all of your friends have mates. The sacrifice you make today (to heal from your past wounds, get therapy if needed, taking a break from dating, self-love) will payoff later. A happier, mental and emotional healthier you will attract the same. "If you don't sacrifice for what you want, what you want will be the sacrifice."

The perfect picture of peace

I'm not sure who first wrote this story, but I think it's a great representation of what peace looks like. "An artist was commissioned by a wealthy man to paint something that would depict peace. After a great deal of thought, the artist painted a beautiful country scene. There were green fields with cows standing in them, birds were flying in the blue sky and a lovely little village lay in a distant valley. The artist gave the picture to the man, but there was a look of disappointment on his face. The man said to the artist, "This isn't a picture of true peace. It isn't right. Go back and try again.

The artist went back to his studio, thought for several hours about peace, then went to his canvas and began to paint. When he was finished, there on the canvas was a beautiful picture of a mother, holding a sleeping baby in her arms, smiling lovingly at the child. He thought, surely, this is true peace, and hurried to give the picture to the wealthy man. But again, the wealthy man refused the painting and asked the painter to try again.

The artist returned again to his studio. He was discouraged, he was tired and he was disappointed. Anger swelled inside him, he felt the rejection of this wealthy man. Again, he thought, he even prayed for inspiration to paint a picture of true peace. Then, all of a sudden, an idea came, he rushed to the canvas and began to paint as he had never painted before. When he finished, he hurried to the wealthy man.

He gave the painting to the man. He studied it carefully for several minutes. The artist held his breath. Then the wealthy man said, "Now this is a picture of true peace." He accepted the painting, paid the artist and everyone was happy.

And what was this picture of true peace?? The picture showed a stormy sea pounding against a cliff. The artist had captured the furry of the wind as it whipped black rain clouds which were laced with streaks of lightening. The sea was roaring in turmoil, waves churning, the dark sky filled with the power of the furious thunderstorm.

And in the middle of the picture, under a cliff, the artist had painted a small bird, safe and dry in her nest snuggled safely in the rocks. The bird was at peace midst the storm that raged about her." What this story tells us is the storms in life will come, but it's how we handle the storms and handle ourselves during the storm that determines whether or not we are in a state of peace.

When the storms hit, be like the palm tree

I'm sure you've heard someone say, "One thing about storms, either you're in a storm, just coming out of a storm, or soon enough, you'll be heading into a storm." When you are in storm, don't be like an oak tree or a pine tree – they break. Be like the palm tree. Have you noticed that during a hurricane, the palm tree bends – bends a lot, but what it doesn't do is break.

Palm trees have a large number of short roots spread across the upper levels of the soil, which work to secure a large amount of soil around the root ball. The stem of a palm tree is made of many small bundles of woody material, which is like bundles of wires inside a telephone cable. During the storm, you might look at the palm tree flattened against the ground and think it's never going to stand upright again, but when the storm dies down, the palm tree is actually able to stand upright again. It comes back from the storm better and stronger than ever. So, when the storms come in your life, be like the palm tree and remember that although you may bend, don't break. If you just hold on, you will come out of the storm stronger than you were before.

Tips to live your life to the fullest

Steve Jobs said it best when he said, "Your time is limited, don't waste it living someone else's life. Don't be trapped by dogma, which is living the result of other people's thinking. Don't let the noise of other's opinion drown your own inner voice. And most important, have the courage to follow your heart and intuition, they somehow already know what you truly want to become. Everything else is secondary." I want to share 20 tips to help you live your best life now.

1. **Be committed to your growth. Set goals and write them down.** Add timelines to your goals (e.g., weeks, months, year). Know what you want to achieve for each stretch of your life, and make sure to look back and see if you actually made the progress you wanted. Keep in mind that your list

will evolve over time. Writing down your goals makes them visible and you are more like to achieve them when you are able to see them on paper.

2. **Discover your life purpose and live in alignment with that purpose.** Set the mission statement for your life, next, outline how you can live your life in way that is true to your purpose.

3. **Live in the moment. Fully embrace the now.** Participate in life instead of just watching it pass by. Be completely immersed in the moment and don't sleepwalk your life away. Don't be held back by what happened yesterday, the day before, the week before, the year before, or even decades ago. Life is short, so live in the present moment.

4. **Don't live for others.** Stop trying to please other people or to be someone else. Don't choose your path in life based on the expectations set on you by others.
5. **Love yourself.** You have to love yourself before someone else can love you. Self-love is so important.
6. **Act like a kid.** Yes, you read that right. This thing called adulting can be overwhelming at times. Kids have a way of enjoying life. Simple things like riding their bike or hanging out with friends make them happy. It's okay to be silly sometimes. Have fun!
7. **Determine your values.** What are your core values? Your core values are the beliefs that shape who you are and how you live your life.

Reflecting on your values will help you set goals for yourself that are "value-congruent," You are more likely to feel fulfilled and happy when you're living in accordance with your values.

8. **Quit complaining.** How much time do you spend complaining about your problems instead of trying to fix them? Instead of complaining, fix the things you can change and learn to ignore the things you can't change.

9. **Be flexible.** We become frustrated because we expect things to stay the same or we expect things to happen overnight. However, life is full of change. Open yourself to the processes of change and growth, and learn to adapt to the new situations and challenges that happen.

10. **Be an optimist.** Instead of being the glass half empty type, see the glass as half full. Don't obsess over bad news; instead, focus your attention on areas of your life that you are profoundly grateful.

11. **Hang out with people who bring you higher.** There are a lot of energy-suckers in the world, so it's important to hang out with people who are filled with positive energy. Hang around with people who bring you higher and not bring you down. You are the average of the five people you spend the most time with. Choose wisely.

12. **Design your ideal life.** If you don't know what you want, it's easy to go through life on auto-pilot. Your first step is to figure out what you want from life. Once you figure out what you

want, create a plan to attain your ideal life and then EXECUTE!

13. **Create your own opportunities.** You can wait for opportunities to find you or you can go out there and create your own opportunities.

14. **Let go of relationships that do not serve you.** That means letting go of people who bring out the worst in you. If the relationship is preventing you from growing, let it go.

15. **Help others live their best life.** One of the greatest joys in life is to give and know that you've made a difference in someone's life.

16. **Push yourself out of your comfort zone.** Research shows that people need to push themselves beyond their comfort zone to perform at their best.

17. **Stop giving up**. Have you seen the picture of the man who was digging his way out underground and he gave up? In the picture you could see that he was so close to the end. Had he just kept going, he would've reached his destination. Things are always hard until they get better, but you'll never know how close you came to achieving your goals if you quit before you see them all the way through.

18. **Simplify your life.** Your possessions can end up possessing you. The less you need to be happy, the happier you'll be.

19. **Write a letter to your future self.** We've heard of people writing letters to their 20-year old self or teenage self, but we don't hear many people writing a letter to their future self. Envision how

you'll be in the future, one year from now. Write that. Seal it and put it in a safe place. Set a calendar reminder one year from now, so you'll know to open when it's time.

20. **Practice an attitude of gratitude**. We ALL have something to be grateful for. Research shows that practicing gratitude makes you feel healthier, happier, and more positive

21 Days to Living a Life by Design

Change doesn't happen overnight. For change to be lasting, there's a process you must go through. The rest of this book is a 21-day-by-day journey to living your life by design. Why 21 days? Because it has been said that if you do something for 21 days, it becomes habit.

In this section of the book, I ask you to write your responses below each day's question. Psychologists believe that writing helps you be reflective AND you tend to remember what you write. Writing things down:

- Clears your mind for higher level thinking.
- Helps your process emotions.
- Gives you a record of the past.
- Makes you more committed.
- Helps clarify your intentions and goals.
- Keeps you motivated.
- Encourages daily progress.

If you prefer, you can write in a journal instead.

Day 1: Self-Assessment

Action Item: Answer the question, "Who are you?" Write a one-page summary of how you see yourself.

_____

_____

_____

_____

_____

_____

_____

_____

_____

_____

_____

_____

_____

Day 2: What negative patterns or habits continue to manifest themselves in your life? (Think about the last five years)

_____

_____

_____

_____

_____

_____

_____

_____

_____

_____

_____

_____

_____

Day 3: Thinking about the last year, what were your biggest disappointments?

_____
_____
_____
_____
_____
_____
_____
_____
_____
_____
_____
_____

Day 4: Thinking about the last year, what were your biggest accomplishments?

_____

_____

_____

_____

_____

_____

_____

_____

_____

_____

_____

_____

_____

Day 5: Think about a time when you were most at peace. What did that time look like?

Day 6: What do you want most in your life? What do you want more of in the future?

_____
_____
_____
_____
_____
_____
_____
_____
_____
_____
_____
_____

Day 7: Are your finances where you want to be? Do you have financial fears? What is your financial plan for the future?

_____

_____

_____

_____

_____

_____

_____

_____

_____

_____

_____

_____

_____

Day 8: What relationships in your life bring out the worst in you? What relationships bring out the best in you? What are the common characteristics of the good and bad? Answering this will help you determine the type of people you need more in your life and those you need less in your life.

_____

_____
_____
_____
_____
_____
_____
_____

Day 9: What are five to ten things you can do to achieve the things you said you wanted most on Day 6?

_____

_____

_____

_____

_____

_____

_____

_____

_____

_____

_____

_____

_____

Day 10: What are your three biggest goals for the next year? What steps are you going to take to make each goal a reality?

_____

_____

_____

_____

_____

_____

_____

_____

_____

_____

_____

_____

Day 11: What is your mission statement for your life?

Day 12: What are the five things you fear or doubt most about your future? If you have less than five, that's great.

_____

_____

_____

_____

_____

_____

_____

_____

_____

_____

_____

_____

Day 13: What is your why? What's your life purpose? What gifts do you have that aid you in walking more in your purpose?

_____

_____

_____

_____

_____

_____

_____

_____

_____

_____

_____

_____

Day 14: What did you do today to move closer to your life's goal(s)?

Day 15: How do you feel about your discovery so far? Have you learned something new about yourself? Has anything changed in your life since day one?

_____

_____

_____

_____

_____

_____

_____

_____

_____

_____

_____

Day 16: Write six positive things about yourself. What makes you the awesome person that you are.

Day 17: On day 7, you outlined your financial plan for the future. What changes have you made in the last 10 days to help you achieve your financial goals? Have you checked your credit score? Are you using a budgeting tool to help you identify where your money is going?

_____

_____

_____

_____

_____

_____

_____

_____

_____

_____

_____

Day 18: Thinking about your goals and plan for your life, do you have people who can help you achieve your goals? If so, who are they and how can they help? If not, what type of people do you need on your "team"?

_____
_____
_____
_____
_____
_____
_____
_____
_____
_____
_____

Day 19: What did you do today to help someone else? Helping others has a positive effect on your life.

_____
_____
_____
_____
_____
_____
_____
_____
_____
_____
_____
_____
_____
_____

Day 20: Thinking about THIS moment, answer the following questions: Where am I right now? Where do I want to go? What steps can I take to get there?

_____
_____
_____
_____
_____
_____
_____
_____
_____
_____
_____

Day 21: Reflecting over the last 21 days, what are the top five things you are grateful for? It's important to practice gratitude daily?

About the Author

Nicole L. Turner is known as the Detox Strategist. As a Detox Strategist, Nicole helps individuals and organizations identify the toxicities in their individual lives, relationships, and organizations that are preventing them from reaching their full potential and helps them develop the strategy and framework they need to reach their goals.

Nicole is available for speaking engagements, seminars, and as a corporate consultant. She can be reached at https://www.detoxstrategist.com/ or https://www.oyatgroup.com/

www.ingramcontent.com/pod-product-compliance
Lightning Source LLC
Chambersburg PA
CBHW061511040426
42450CB00008B/1568